{ ULTIMATE }

CONNECTION

Eight Principles That
Will Transform Your Prayer Life

Barbara Ho

PRAYERSHOP
PUBLISHING

Terre Haute, Indiana

PrayerShop Publishing is the publishing arm of Harvest Prayer Ministries and the Church Prayer Leaders Network. Harvest Prayer Ministries exists to transform lives through teaching prayer. Its online store, www.prayershop.org, has more than 600 prayer resources available for purchase.

ISBN: 978-1-935012-25-2

1 2 3 4 5 | 2015 2014 2013 2012 2011

ACKNOWLEDGEMENTS

I'D LIKE TO EXPRESS HOW GRATEFUL I am to God for giving me this passion for prayer. I truly consider it a precious gift. Your faithfulness never ceases to amaze me.

I'm also thankful for Danny, my very best friend and soul mate for more than 30 years. Your walk of faith blesses me every day and your constant support and encouragement are my rock! I love you!

Thank you also to my niece Heather. I don't know if you really understand how instrumental you were in the writing of this book! You not only encouraged me when things seemed overwhelming, but you took me by the hand and walked this novice writer through the difficult moments. I deeply appreciate you! I can't wait to read your books!

And finally, I'd like to thank my editor Janet Dixon and Prayer-Shop publishers, namely Jon Graf. You were all so great to work with! Thank you for all you've done!

TABLE OF CONTENTS

INTRODUCTION

I WAS SIX MONTHS PREGNANT AND MY winter jacket no longer fit. As my husband, Danny, and I walked through Sears and Roebuck, we noticed what seemed to be the perfect coat. It was $69 and with tax it would cost $75. It might as well have cost $1,000. Danny was in seminary and we barely had enough money to pay our monthly bills. We left the store empty-handed.

In the car driving home, we lifted up the situation to the Lord. On the way back to our apartment, we stopped to check our mail. To our amazement, there was an envelope in our mailbox. No, it did not have cash in it—that would have been spent on more pressing bills. It contained an anonymous gift certificate to Sears for $75. We got back in our car and bought my beautiful new coat!

I was twenty-three years old then and answers like that to prayer have led me to a life of learning to call out to God. I've seen countless answers to prayer and some that have yet to be answered. But I have never seen God fail me, not once! I may not have been privy to everything he was doing at every exact moment, but in hindsight I must say that in every situation God has always been faithful. He has never deserted me but instead has worked each concern for good. He has always been true to his word!

I believe in prayer. I'm convinced that prayer does move the hand of God. Yes, it changes who we are, but it also changes our world, sometimes in a powerful way. As much as I believe in prayer, I believe more in him to whom my prayers are sent. He speaks; we listen. He moves; we obey.

I've had the privilege of seeing many others grow in their prayer lives as I've grown in mine. It's a learning process that takes time. But as the saying goes, "Anything worth having is worth the wait."

This book contains eight principles of prayer that have transformed my life and, I am convinced, can transform yours. These are not complicated. They are instead practical, life-changing concepts that will lead you into a step-by-step life of exciting and fruitful prayer.

Chapter 1

MY LIFE OF PRAYER

I'VE LIVED A JOURNEY OF LEARNING TO PRAY. I struggled to spend time with God when my boys were young, trying desperately to squeeze in just a few minutes with the Lord each day. As they grew older, my time was pulled by school outings, homework, church events, and just the everyday life situations of a mom and a pastor's wife.

Since those early years, I've learned not only of the importance of prayer, but what an awesome and yet greatly misunderstood privilege of the Christian life it is. You see, the fact of the matter is, prayer changes things! God changes things! His intention is to use us as tools in his hand. Prayer not only shapes us into those useful tools, but it also actually moves the hands of our creator God.

I love to pray! I love to pray with people and for people. I love to pray aloud and in the quiet of my heart. I especially enjoy praying for groups of people, both large and small. I've seen the Lord answer so many prayers it brings tears to my eyes just thinking about it. Don't get me wrong: I've experienced some of the same struggles many people do when it comes to prayer, but I can honestly say I now have an effective *and enjoyable* prayer life!

Receiving the Principles

Something very strange happened to me about four years ago while I was walking out of a Wal-Mart store. I began to "receive" what I call "prayer principles." I've heard musicians describe receiving a song like this. Some have shared stories where they had to get out of bed and write the lyrics or musical notes to a new song. That's exactly how it happened to me. I hurried to my car and frantically wrote down seven principles of prayer on a paper napkin. As I later looked over what I had written, I realized that these are foundational principles I've used in my prayer life. The Lord had given me a blessed gift and I knew it. I later added an eighth principle and throughout the next several years I've asked the Lord for direction as to what to do with what he had given me.

Although I've had numerous opportunities to speak and teach about them, it wasn't until recently that I've been impressed to put them in a book. When the Lord began to place this on my heart, I laughed! "I can't write a book! That's crazy!" I said. But I soon surrendered to his leading and here I am. One thing I do know: these principles are from the Lord. Simply put, these are eight aspects of prayer that, if incorporated as we pray, will have a transforming effect on our prayer lives.

Longing for a Connection with God

Today, more than ever, people are struggling with the issue of prayer. If you want to speak at a workshop and have it filled, speak about prayer. It's a hot topic in Christian circles. Many are longing for an intimate connection with God but frankly don't know how to get it! "If God is who the Bible says he is, why don't we see more answers to our prayers?" they ask. "When we pray for people to be healed, why do so many seem to go unanswered?"

In 2005, LifeWay Christian Resources did a worldwide study of more than 1,300 evangelical leaders to see what they perceived to be the "Top 10 Issues Facing Today's Church." Not surprising to me, prayer topped the list as number one. Although people seem interested in prayer, over my past thirty years in ministry, I've personally seen a decline in both the quality and quantity of the time people spend in prayer. Many people seem unfulfilled when it comes to prayer. Few actually pray on a daily basis. I'm here to say this does not have to be so! God intends us to connect deeply with him, and prayer is one of the main ways we do that. Our prayer times can and should be a response to a deep need and desire, not a reaction to a sense of obligation or guilt.

God wants to meet each of us in prayer. He wants not only to hear *from* us, but he wants to *speak to* us. One of the most common questions I hear is "How do I know God is speaking to me?" I've been asked to describe the sound of his voice. "How does he speak?" "How does he lead?" "What if what I'm hearing is not his voice?" These eight principles answer these and many other prayer-related questions.

Learning to Pray

Let's face it; praying consistently can be tough! If you're like me, you've struggled to spend time in prayer. Maybe you've experienced negative emotions such as guilt, frustration, and disappointment when it comes to your prayer life. I know I have! I remember numerous times crying before the Lord and confessing my lack of prayer. I was often one of those people filling workshops with the intention of growing in my prayer life. I've longed for a deeper intimate relationship with God.

From many conversations with others, I can assure you we're not alone! I believe you've picked up this book about prayer for a reason. I don't know you or your story, but do I know God! I know he can change your prayer life into a vibrant, blessed, awesome daily experience. I know that your prayers can change lives for eternity and that God can use you to make a difference in a world that greatly needs the touch of the Savior. He's worked in amazing ways in my life and I'm confident he can work in yours!

Do you believe that? I do! Jeremiah 32:27 says, "I am the LORD, the God of all mankind. Is anything too hard for me?" Learning to pray means learning to place all our trust in both who God is and what he can do. It's keeping our eyes off *our* limitations and focusing on *his* limitless abilities!

As you read this book, be warned: my prayer for you is that God will shake things up and lead you into a life of radical prayer, that you'll experience a taste of what God can do both in and through you. I've seen God answer prayers that have shaken my world. He is, after all, the creator God. He also is our Abba Father, who loves us with an everlasting love! "So I say to you: Ask and it will be given to you; seek and you will find; knock and the door will be opened to you. For everyone who asks receives; he who seeks finds; and to him who knocks, the door will be opened" (Luke 11:9-10).

The following pages are the culmination of eight principles of prayer that have absolutely transformed my prayer life. Keep in mind that although the principles are listed and described separately in each of the following chapters, all need to be working together. This is by no means a formula. It's merely the heartfelt sharing of my life of prayer.

Discussion Questions

1. On a scale from 1 to 10 (10 being "excellent"), how would you rate the quality of your time in prayer? What could you do to improve your score?

2. What would you say is your biggest hindrance in your prayer life? What practical steps could you take to overcome this problem?

3. What are some common reasons people struggle with prayer?

4. What is your favorite part of prayer, and why? What is your least favorite part, and why?

5. What changes would you like to see in your prayer life as a result of reading this book?

Prayer Action Step

Begin keeping a prayer journal as you read and study this book. Be sure to include the date of each entry as well as the things you're learning and particular issues God is speaking to you about. Be specific. Expect God to speak and be prepared to receive.

If you're in a group, pray for one another that each person would grow greatly in his prayer life as he reads this. If you're studying this alone, ask God to open your heart to learn and grow in this mighty area of prayer. And finally, commit each principle to memory. It's important to allow each one to take root.

Chapter 2

Principle 1:

WE ARE DESPERATE FOR GOD

HAVE YOU EVER FELT TOTALLY DESPERATE? Perhaps you have been desperate for comfort after the painful death of someone you love. Others may be in desperate need of healing from the effects of sickness and pain. I have never experienced desperation to this extent, but I know many who have.

Desperation is a great motivator. People will go to almost any extreme when they are desperate. When terrorists attacked the World Trade Center on 9/11, our son was employed by a company located only a few blocks away. Because of the situation, no cell connections were available. We, along with our new daughter-in-law, Laura, had no communication with him throughout much of the day. I can tell you, we would have done almost anything to hear from him. You could say we were desperate to hear his voice, and when we did, we were elated!

Let me ask you: how desperate are you for God? Are you desperate for his touch? Do you long to hear his voice? Unless the Lord rescues, we have no hope! Do you believe that, really? Do your prayers reflect that sense of complete desperation?

The foundation of our prayers needs to be laid on a deep-rooted awareness that only God can meet our needs and that his touch is the only thing that can bring a much-needed change.

Often I hear of people "trying" to pray for a particular situation. It's almost like trying on an outfit to see if it fits, only to quickly take it back if it doesn't. That's not effective prayer! Our prayers need to be filled with undying commitment. We need to come before the Lord's presence in full surrender. During one of her conferences, Beth Moore, one of my favorite speakers and authors, talked about lying facedown on the floor in prayer with her arms outstretched. What a beautiful description of desperation before God!

Psalm 127:1 describes the mind-set we must embrace as we enter into prayer with the Lord:

> Unless the LORD builds the house, its builders labor
> in vain.
> Unless the LORD watches over the city, the watch-
> men stand guard in vain.

Literally all of our confidence has to be in God and in the expectation of his answer to our prayer. We have to be fully aware of the fact that there's nothing we can do. We have no power to change whatever situation we're facing, but God does—and he will!

Push Through the Crowd

One of my favorite passages of Scripture is Mark 5:24-34:

A large crowd followed and pressed around him. And a woman was there who had been subject to bleeding for twelve years. She had suffered a great deal under the care of many doctors and had spent all she had, yet instead of getting better she grew worse. When she heard about Jesus, she came up behind him in the crowd and touched his cloak, because she thought, "If I just touch his clothes, I will be healed." Immediately her bleeding stopped and she felt in her body that she was freed from her suffering.

At once Jesus realized that power had gone out from him. He turned around in the crowd and asked, "Who touched my clothes?"

"You see the people crowding against you," his disciples answered, "and yet you can ask, 'Who touched me?'"

But Jesus kept looking around to see who had done it. Then the woman, knowing what had happened to her, came and fell at his feet and, trembling with fear, told him the whole truth. He said to her, "Daughter, your faith has healed you. Go in peace and be freed from your suffering."

The woman in this story perfectly describes this principle of prayer. She was desperate for a touch from the Lord and she knew it! "If I just touch his clothes, I will be healed." Have you ever thought about how difficult it must have been for this woman, most likely weak from bleeding for so many years, to fight her way through the crowd to touch the Lord? There were so many people in the crowd that when Jesus asked his disciples who had touched him, they basically said, "Are you kidding? There are too many people around you to tell you that!" Yet this woman didn't let anyone or anything stop her because she knew how to receive her much-needed healing!

I can't tell you how many times I've pictured myself fighting my way through a crowd to touch Jesus during a particular prayer time. I often declare, "Lord, I am pushing through this crowd of fear (or lack of faith, or bitterness, or whatever is hindering me from receiving from God what I need) and I am claiming the victory! I am clinging to you, and no one or nothing is standing in my way!"

When was the last time you fought your way through the crowd to touch the Lord? Why don't we reach out to him in this way more often? I believe it's because we're not *desperate* for his touch, not really!

After the attacks of 9/11, people were desperate for the Lord. Many were reaching out to God for comfort, for answers, for stability. The night after the bombings, our church called together a prayer meeting, as did many churches throughout the country. The place was full! People came out to pray as never before. I cannot remember such great attendance for prayer in our church's history. Many who had never attended a prayer meeting came out and literally cried out to God. It was awesome to see people reaching out to the Lord.

The following week, the numbers dropped a bit, but still more than usual came out to pray. Within the weeks that followed, though, the numbers dwindled back to the same folks who came to pray before the tragedy happened. I believe that initially, people realized how much they needed help from the Lord. Within time, they forgot their need for God and went back to their normal lives. Desperation for God was replaced with their busy lifestyles. I guess the crowd was too large to overcome. What a shame!

Five Minutes or Full Commitment?

The most important aspect of this principle of desperation for God is humility. As we come before the throne of grace, we must keep in mind that we are nothing without his intervention. Our attitude has to be "Whatever, whenever, if ever, Lord." It's all up to God! It doesn't matter if our request is as big as praying for the healing of a dying friend, or as seemingly small as asking for grace in a shopping adventure—we need to be humbled before an all-powerful, all-knowing, all-caring God!

I remember an incident that happened in my life more than fifteen years ago. It was Sunday morning and I was getting myself and my two sons ready for church. While I was getting dressed, I sensed the Holy Spirit calling me to spend time with him. Wanting to take enough time to look my best, I told him that I would answer his call as I drove to pick a friend up for church. That would give me fifteen minutes, which should be more than enough time to spend in prayer! I finished getting ready, started my car, and even turned off my radio. How much more committed could I be? As I waited for his sweet presence, there was an obvious deadness in the car. "Lord," I complained, "you've been calling me all morning to spend time with you, and here I am! Where are you?"

The Lord spoke a word of rebuke to me that day that I will never forget. "I am the Lord! You will either put me first in your life or don't put me at all!" I spent the next few minutes in confession as I wept before the Lord. I learned a great lesson that day about who God is! I learned how important it is to be desperate for him, really desperate. I can't fully describe to you how much this incident has affected my prayer life. He longs for us to be in communion and prayer with him, but this communion involves the deep understanding of our desperation and complete need for him. Once we've really grasped that concept in our hearts and minds, it must flow out of our prayers.

I recently visited my favorite online Christian bookstore and typed the words "five minutes" into the search bar. It brought me to a whole page of DVDs and books—including devotionals and books on prayer—offering to transform my life in five minutes. I know we're a busy society, but *five minutes*? Where's the desperation there? The unfortunate thing is that the authors know that if they can get people to pray and read the Bible for five minutes a day, that's progress! Their hearts are right. It just saddens me at the small amount of time people are willing to spend with God on a daily basis.

Praying with the full understanding of our desperation for the Lord reaps great blessings. When we're willing to "put it all on the line," God has an opportunity to pour his grace into whatever situation we're praying for. He wants to answer our prayers, but he will only answer when we are totally and completely desperate for him.

Discussion Questions

A large crowd followed and pressed around him. And a woman was there who had been subject to bleeding for twelve years. She had suffered a great deal under the care of many doctors and had spent all she had, yet instead of getting better she grew worse. When she heard about Jesus, she came up behind him in the crowd and touched his cloak, because she thought, "If I just touch his clothes, I will be healed." Immediately her bleeding stopped and she felt in her body that she was freed from her suffering. (Mark 5:24-29)

1. How would you define the word "desperate" in the context of your relationship with God and your prayer life?

2. Why is desperation for the Lord's touch so important? In practical terms, what would desperation look like in your prayer life?

3. Why was it so important for the woman in Mark to literally touch the Lord Jesus?

4. How can you touch the Lord in your prayers?

5. What are some "crowds" you need to overcome that can prevent you from touching God during your prayer times?

Prayer Action Step

What one change can you make this week enabling your prayers to reflect more desperation for God? Do you need to spend more time with the Lord? Are you allowing life situations to drown out your relationship with him? Is fear limiting your prayer life?

If you're studying in a group, share some of these needed changes with each other and then pray for one another. Determine this week to live out these changes. If you're doing this study alone, write down the specific areas of desperation God is speaking to you about. Commit these to him and trust him to work them out in your life!

Chapter 3

Principle 2:

GOD EXISTS

HEBREWS 11:6 TELLS US, "Without faith it is impossible to please God, because anyone who comes to him *must believe that he exists* and that he rewards those who earnestly seek him." It seems obvious that a person praying would be aware of the fact that God exists! After all, why would you pray unless you knew you were praying to God? This may sound simple, but I've found this to be one of the hardest principles for people to practice.

So much of our understanding of who God is comes into play in this principle. Let's face it: it takes faith to believe there's a God who has been there forever, who will never die, and who created the universe with a word! This is not your run-of-the-mill concept. Yet it's the foundation of our prayer lives!

Dependence on God

Dependence is the key to our concept of who we really believe God is. If I'm praying for a sick person and I'm not convinced that I'm praying to a healing God, my prayers will be ineffective. The same is true when praying for favor in your finances. Do we really believe we're praying to Jehovah-Jireh, our God who provides?

One of the main struggles we face when we pray is, as Proverbs 3:5 describes, "leaning not on our own understanding." This is key to an effective prayer life. Our tendency is to try to figure things out ourselves and then, on the basis of that understanding, to take whatever steps we think we need to take. What we're saying when we do this is "I am more able than God is to take care of this situation. I don't need him!" There's no way we can think we are better able to control our lives and at the same time really believe God is who he says he is. "I am the LORD, the God of all mankind. Is anything too hard for me?" (Jeremiah 32:27). Of course when things don't work out, we often turn to him and "allow" or even beg him to intervene. When we fully acknowledge who God is, we should have no choice but to trust in him and surrender whatever situation we're praying for into his sovereign hands!

People can disbelieve that God exists even in answered prayer. How many times have I seen the obvious hand of God in a particular situation, only to have the person involved chalk it up to good fortune or "blessed chance"? I want to scream out, "That was God! Give him the glory!"

I recently stepped on a fire ant hill. Now, for those of you who live in the southern part of the U.S., you will understand why I panicked when I looked down and saw my foot completely covered in fire ants. Let's just say I did a little jig! While I was shaking these ants off, I prayed and cried out to God, "Lord, help these ants not to bite me." Well, for about an hour I felt like my foot was on fire! It literally made me sick to my stomach. But the incredible thing was that after that first hour, the ant bites never affected me. They turned red and festered with white blisters for the next two weeks, but the effects never bothered me. I could attribute that to good fortune, but I know God granted favor! He answered my prayer as they were biting. I believe I received a miracle that day.

Unfortunately, this refusal to acknowledge God's hand working is not only true for those who don't know the Lord in a personal way, but to those who serve and love him. Why is it so hard to see God's hand in a situation? Maybe he provided a much-needed job, or spared you from an almost deadly car crash, or maybe he protected you from the painful effects of fire ant bites. This is "not believing God exists" in its simplest form. If we really believe God exists, we will see his hand working in our daily lives.

What joy and freedom this principle brings. It's a relief to surrender my requests to a God who not only exists but who is, as the Bible states, "able to do immeasurably more than all we ask or imagine" (Ephesians 3:20).

Keep Your Focus on God

One of the transforming aspects of this principle that God exists deals with where we keep our focus. As we pray, we need to keep our focus on God. Picture him. Remind yourself of his character traits. Think of him as he was on the earth. What kind of a man was he? How did he deal with people?

Recently, I struggled with a tough relationship issue. Fear was at my doorstep. Could I trust God to meet this need, really? I decided I needed to understand more of what kind of a man Jesus was in order to trust him in this relational struggle. I began an in-depth study of the gospel of Matthew. I carefully studied how, as a man, Jesus ministered to people. I was reminded of his compassion when he cared for the hungry crowd and fed the 5,000; his tenderheartedness as he touched and healed the leper; and his love for the poor as he taught the Beatitudes. Reading each day about his life gave me confidence that he was, and is, someone I can fully trust.

As I prayed about this over the next few weeks, fear concerning this particular relationship was replaced by peace and confidence that God was in control. In every situation for prayer, whether great or small, we will be faced with the choice either to acknowledge the existence and control of God or to allow ourselves to be in control. It's important to keep our focus glued on the existence of God! Second Corinthians 10:5 describes this: "We demolish arguments and every pretension that sets itself up against the knowledge of God, and we take captive every thought to make it obedient to Christ."

When I'm going through one of these times, I picture Jesus in my mind. I begin quoting scriptures that support the victory I need in whatever situation I'm facing. For example, if I am dealing with a fear, I might claim Psalm 27:1:

> The LORD is my light and my salvation—
> whom shall I fear?
> The LORD is the stronghold of my life—
> of whom shall I be afraid?

The existence of God changes everything. Imagine a place without his presence. It would be a pretty miserable place. When we pray we need to remind ourselves of his existence. When we're aware that the Lord is with us, we act differently. Our thoughts are different. Our concerns are different. I don't know about you, but when I am aware of the fact that God is present, I'm not only more careful of how I act, but I'm not afraid. I'm at peace. This has to be the way it is when we pray. It's easy to get caught up in mindless, mundane praying. When we pray, are we convinced that we are in the presence of the risen Christ? Do we see his hand at work in our daily lives? That is what makes all the difference!

I can share from experience that as we practice choosing to keep our thoughts, our emotions, and our focus on the existence of God, we will have victory in our prayer lives. What an awesome God we serve! Don't let the enemy or the world steal the joy of this principle from you!

Discussion Questions

And without faith it is impossible to please God, because anyone who comes to him *must believe that he exists* and that he rewards those who earnestly seek him. (Hebrews 11:6)

1. According to Hebrews 11:6, what is necessary to please God? How can you demonstrate this characteristic?

2. How might your prayers reflect belief in the existence of God and yet deny that he rewards you when you seek him?

3. What does it mean to earnestly seek God?

4. How can you more earnestly seek him?

5. How do you think God rewards you when you earnestly seek him?

Prayer Action Step

Think of a time when the existence of God made a difference in your life. Write it down and describe how things might have been different if he hadn't intervened. If you never have, take the time to thank the Lord for his presence at that time in your life.

If you're in a group, briefly describe this time. Whether in a group or alone, spend some time praying and asking God to give you a keener awareness of his existence.

Chapter 4

Principle 3:

GOD ANSWERS THE PRAYERS OF FAITH

THE NEW INTERNATIONAL VERSION OF THE BI-BLE uses the word "faith" more than 400 times! Faith is a small but powerful word. Hebrews 11:6 teaches that "without faith it is impossible to please God." Let me reword that. If we're not practicing faith in our lives, we are displeasing the Lord! Too often we live as though walking in faith were an option, some kind of special ability given to a few rare souls. It's not! We're called and expected to live a life of faith, and that needs to play out most of all in our prayer lives.

I love studying Hebrews 11. It's my favorite chapter in the Bible! In case you're not familiar with it, it's referred to as the "faith chapter." I've read it so many times that my pages are thinned out. I have markings on many of the verses. It begins in verse 1 by defining faith: "Faith is being sure of what we hope for and certain of what we do not see."

"Sure of what we hope for"! What an amazing statement. Faith is living out trust in God! It's walking and making decisions with the certainty that the creator God is in control. One of my favorite sayings is "Faith is not believing God can, it's knowing he will!" It's being confident that he wants the best for us and living with that assurance. Does that sound too simple to you? We tend to think of faith as a supernatural happening when all of a sudden our emotions soar to the sky and we're caught up in this moment of belief. Those times may happen on occasion, but I believe they're rare! Faith is a daily lifestyle of choosing to trust God.

What Faith Looks Like

If you read through the great heroes of faith listed in Hebrews 11, you'll notice something interesting. "By faith" every person took the steps that he took.

> By faith Abel offered God a better sacrifice than
> Cain did. (11:4)
> By faith Noah . . . built an ark to save his family.
> (11:7)
> By faith Moses . . . refused to be known as the son of
> Pharaoh's daughter. (11:24)
> By faith the people passed through the Red Sea as on
> dry land. (11:29)
> By faith the walls of Jericho fell, after the people had
> marched around them for seven days. (11:30)

The amazing thing about all these saints was not only their faith, but that their faith led to action and victory! Many of us will acknowledge how awesome God is, but it's a different story to step out and act on it. Now *that's* faith! Our faith is the key that enables us to victoriously go through whatever situation we're struggling with. It's all about our faith in the Lord!

Day-to-Day Faith

Many Christians tend to look for what I call the "wow factor" in their Christian lives, including when they pray. They expect their spiritual growth to come out of mountaintop experiences, often during a Christian retreat, when something sensational has happened in their life, or after God has spoken to them in a powerful way. I've seen even pastors get pulled into this way of thinking. Every meeting has to be amazing. Every encounter must be powerful.

In the same way, many expect their faith to grow from highly emotional events. Now, these times do happen. They've happened in my Christian walk and I look forward to them happening again. They are indeed wonderful and God-given. But it is not during these times that we grow the most. Our growth happens primarily in our day-by-day life experiences, both pleasant and unpleasant. Faith is like a muscle that takes time to build. If you've ever been involved in working out, you've seen how slowly these muscles grow with daily exercising. As we begin making life choices based on godly direction, things begin to happen. Eventually, we look in the mirror and see real definition. Our foundation of faith gradually grows so it will be strong and ready for the big moments. We need to commit to the long haul and know that God is working in our lives. Slowly but surely, our faith will grow, in time!

Many of the choices of faith listed in Hebrews 11 would be considered normal life choices to most people. Think about it. Moses' parents were mentioned because they hid Moses for three months. This due to the fact that they "saw he was no ordinary child" (11:23). How is that faith? Where's the explosive moment? They chose to hide their son to protect him. What parent wouldn't do that? Well, it seems, according to historical accounts, that many parents wouldn't! The fact is they were acting in faith because they trusted that God had given them a special son and took steps to protect him. Because they disobeyed the king's edict, they faced the danger of losing their own lives and the life of their son as well. But their faith in God outweighed the dangers they faced.

How about Abraham? He was highlighted because he obeyed the Lord and "made his home in the promised land like a stranger in a foreign country" (11:9). Moving to a new place sounds like everyday living to me. But to Abraham it was a major life change and a direct act of obedience to God. He stepped out in faith! That is what makes Abraham such an amazing example.

Esau's mention of faith was blessing his own sons. And Jacob's step of faith was blessing his grandsons. These seemingly everyday life experiences were nonetheless lived out in steps of faith, faith that played out daily in these saints' lives.

Walking in faith must become a habit, like using a muscle continually so it grows and grows! That's why faith is described in the Bible as a mustard seed. This tiny seed is able to grow into a very large tree!

When Our Faith Is Tested

We will all have those times in our lives when our faith will be tested. It's at those times when the depth of our faith is revealed. In the book of Genesis, God told Abraham to go to Mount Moriah and sacrifice his son Isaac—Issac, who was the miraculous fulfillment of a great promise God had given Abraham about blessing his future generations! Eventually the Lord intervened and provided another sacrifice for Abraham, but he acted on what God told him to do and prepared to offer his son to God on the altar. Think about it: how easy would it have been for Abraham to have doubted God's promise? The idea of essentially murdering his precious son, the only way to fulfill that promise, must have seemed ridiculous! But thankfully, Abraham was a man of daily faith walking. When this huge test came, he stepped out in faith and received victory.

Be assured of this: God will test our faith. It's not a question of *if*—it's more like *when.* It may not be as difficult as Abraham's test was, but Scripture teaches us that the test will come!

Not every difficult situation is a test of faith, though. Reasons for some may never be known this side of heaven. On March 21, 2008, Steven Curtis Chapman's beautiful daughter was accidentally run over and killed by his teenage son. What a terrible tragedy! Many parents would never be able to cope with an accident like that. But, although I'm sure the pain will never completely leave, Steven and his wife did cope, by the grace and mercy of God.

In the song "Beauty Will Rise," Steven wrote about joy coming in the morning. It's a song of victory and grace. The amazing thing is that he wrote the words after this terrible accident. I can assure you that no one who has not been walking a life of day-by-day faith could ever have experienced what Steven did and still put those words in print.

There come those moments in all believers' lives when we're faced with a decision: will we choose to trust God and stand in faith, or will we allow our flesh to take over? These moments can come either in life-shaking events or in everyday life experiences. Sometimes they come during a phone call, in a crisis, or when faced with financial pressures. Make no mistake—these moments bring about a clear choice.

When we choose the flesh, we focus on the situation and take the pressures of the issue on ourselves. We lean on our own understanding. When we choose this route, negative emotions like fear, bitterness, anger, defeatism, and hopelessness come gushing in like a river. We begin to believe we'll never have victory over the problem. It's too often the road most taken.

When we choose instead to focus on God and give the situation to the Lord, we stand in faith, not giving in to fear or the dread of "what if." It's important to note that the sooner we surrender these situations to God, the less apt we are to experience many of the negative emotions waiting to flood our hearts and minds. The longer we wait, the greater the battle.

During these times of choice, I will often physically stand while I'm praying to show my determination to trust God in this mental battle. I've begun to realize just how much the enemy targets these specific "choice crossroads" in our lives. I can't stress this enough. I have found these critical times of choice between trusting God and our own fleshly understanding to be key opportunities for Satan to try to get a foothold. Instead, let's stand against his wicked schemes and choose to walk in faith!

Praying in Faith

Faith is essential to our walk with Christ and especially our prayer lives. We cannot have an effective prayer life if we are not walking in faith! It's that simple. So what does our enemy do? He attacks our faith. He begins throwing all kinds of lies and confusion into our minds to lead us away from trusting God. He magnifies the possible negative results of the situation to a level of fear: "What am I going to do?" He'll throw in questions of doubt about God: "Does God really want this?" "Did he really say that?" When we begin to doubt the word of the Lord, our faith is shot!

I've come across a teaching in the Christian community that bothers me more than I can say. It says that when we pray, we don't change God as much as it's we ourselves that are changed. It teaches that God will do as God has planned and we don't actually change that, but we should pray because it's good for our spiritual growth!

Let me begin by saying, yes, when we pray, we are changed. How can you not be changed when you speak on a personal level to the creator of the universe? But our prayers *do* move the hand of God. If I didn't believe that, I would never spend as much time in prayer interceding for my needs and for others as I do. My joy comes in knowing that "the prayer of a righteous man is powerful and effective" (James 5:16). Our prayers make a huge difference in our lives, and in the lives of countless others!

Hebrews 11:6 tells us that "without faith it is impossible to please God, because anyone who comes to him must believe that he exists *and that he rewards those who earnestly seek him.*" A key part of faith comes in knowing God will answer us when we pray. How many times do I hear people pray for something and I know by their words they do not expect God to answer, not really? We should take to heart the old saying, "If you're praying for rain, don't forget your umbrella!"

Praying in faith involves praying specifically. This is a huge area that is lacking in most Christians' lives. We tend to pray generally and seldom take a step out and ask the Lord for specific requests. It's almost like we pray for the peripheral and ignore the main problem. Are we in need for finances? Ask God for it. Do we hate our job? Acknowledge it before the Lord and ask for either a new attitude or a new job. How about our relationships—what needs to be changed? Where is our stress coming from? Describe it to the Lord and allow him to work.

Consider the detailed proclamation of faith spoken by the great prophet Elijah. In 1 Kings 17:1, he declared, "As the LORD, the God of Israel, lives, whom I serve, there will be neither dew nor rain in the next few years except at my word." And his words became reality! You can't get more specific than that. In Joshua 6:16, God brought down the walls of Jericho when Joshua commanded the people, "Shout! For the LORD has given you the city!" None of these were general proclamations.

I'm convinced the reason more Christians don't pray specifically is that they lack faith. They want a way out, either for themselves, so they don't look foolish if the prayer is not answered, or for God—as if he needs an escape hatch!

Not many things are as exciting as seeing God answer a specific prayer. The joy overflows. How can we experience the excitement of answered prayer if we never ask for specific needs to be met? James 4:3-4 teaches that "you do not have, because you do not ask. When you do ask, you do not receive, because you ask with wrong motives." Do you have a particular prayer need? Bring it to God. Let's be willing to go out on a limb. He's a big God capable of amazing things!

God also speaks. We need to listen as we pray to be sure we're praying according to his leading. It's way too easy to pray according to what we want. I will delve deeper into this issue of hearing from God more in chapter 6.

Praying for the Sick

When we pray for the sick, we are often faced with a strong temptation to doubt not only God's ability to heal, but also his desire to answer our prayers for healing. But James 5:14-15 tells us, "Is any one of you sick? He should call for the elders of the church to pray over him and anoint him with oil in the name of the Lord. And the prayer offered in faith will make the sick person well; the Lord will raise him up."

I love to pray for the sick! I find such joy in praying for those who are suffering, knowing that there's healing available. I've seen many healings. I've seen the Lord remove headaches, coughs, body aches and more. I'm not writing a thesis on healing. I know there are many theological differences in praying for the sick, but one thing I do know: God heals, maybe not every time, but more times than we're willing to ask and trust him for!

So many people pray timidly for the sick, tiptoeing around asking the Lord to bring healing. Or they pray in generalities: guidance for the doctors, or comfort for those who are ill, or grace to go through what they are going through. Believe me, I know these are all valid requests, but what about praying for the Lord to remove whatever is causing the person pain? Why not ask God to meet this specific need?

This is where everyday faith comes into play. If we're living on the daily premise that God is in control and he wants good for us, praying for the sick is not difficult. If the person is not healed, our faith should not be shattered because its foundation is strong. Frankly, we don't have to know all the answers of why God does or doesn't act in certain ways. Our calling is to trust that he is in control and place our full faith in him!

I remember an incident that happened to my husband a few years ago. He was scheduled to speak at a conference and had a terrible cough that caused him not to be able to speak a full sentence together. He called me and updated me about the situation. Now, we could have said, "Well, it just doesn't seem to be God's will for you to speak." I'm sure the conference people would have understood. But we came before the Lord and prayed against the cough! The amazing thing that was when he stepped up to the podium to speak, the cough completely left. Once he stepped down it continued! This happened every time he spoke during the conference. Was God in control? You bet he was, and our faith grew by leaps and bounds, even though no one but Danny and me knew what had happened!

God Loves to Answer Our Prayers

The Bible is filled with promises about how God loves to answer us. One such is Jeremiah 33:3: "Call to me and I will answer you and tell you great and unsearchable things you do not know." His desire is to bless us and to use us to bless others. This can only happen as we choose to walk a life of faith!

For many years, I've prayed for a verse to claim at the beginning of each new year. It's amazing how the truth of these particular verses unfolds during the coming year. The verse God led me to for 2009 has impacted my life like none other. It's from Ephesians 3:20-21: "Now to him who is able to do immeasurably more than all we ask or imagine, according to his power that is at work within us, to him be glory in the church and in Christ Jesus throughout all generations, for ever and ever! Amen."

I want to close this chapter with this word. God has amazing things prepared for you, things beyond anything you can ever even imagine. I have no idea where your life is, but I know he wants you to live a dynamic and fulfilled life. The key, my friend, is faith. Will you walk in it? The choice is yours.

Discussion Questions

And *without faith it is impossible to please God*, because anyone who comes to him must believe that he exists and that he rewards those who earnestly seek him. (Hebrews 11:6)

1. How would you define "faith"?

2. Why is faith so important in your walk with the Lord?

3. What steps can you take to increase your faith when you find it lacking?

4. What does it mean to "pray in faith"? Will this affect how specifically you pray? If so, how?

5. The enemy is always ready to attack your faith and hinder your prayers. What can you do to stand guard against him?

Prayer Action Step

Think of more ways you can step out in faith as you pray. How can you move away from praying in generalities toward more specific requests? Consider how you can pray more effectively for others on a daily basis.

If you're praying in a group, briefly share some of the changes you want to make and pray for one another. If doing this study alone, take note of the changes God is speaking to you about, then ask and trust him to work his grace in you in order to live out these changes.

Chapter 5

Principle 4:

THE PRAYERS OF THE RIGHTEOUS ARE POWERFUL AND EFFECTIVE

I HAVE CLAIMED THIS VERSE IN PRAYER more times than I can begin to count: "The prayer of a righteous man is powerful and effective" (James 5:16). God answers the prayers of the righteous. I'm reminded of this every time I pray and I often speak it with confidence.

Are you able to pray with confidence, or do you feel too unworthy to have your prayers answered? Can you come boldly before the Lord and bring your concerns and burdens to him, or do you struggle with feelings of condemnation or unworthiness? How can you pray with assurance when you know you're far from perfect?

The Prayers of the *Righteous*

To begin with, our righteousness comes from who we are *in the Lord* and our relationship with him. It's based on what Christ has accomplished on the cross. Once we have surrendered our lives to Christ, we are then free to receive forgiveness for our sins, past, present, and future. He paid the penalty for our sin. That is our firm foundation! "This righteousness from God comes through faith in Jesus Christ to all who believe" (Romans 3:22). We are able to pray in confidence because of our *position* of righteousness in Christ! How freeing this is? I don't have to be perfect to come before the throne of grace. In Hebrews 10:19-23 we read:

> Therefore, brothers, since we have confidence to enter the Most Holy Place by the blood of Jesus, by a new and living way opened for us through the curtain, that is, his body, and since we have a great priest over the house of God, let us draw near to God with a sincere heart in full assurance of faith, having our hearts sprinkled to cleanse us from a guilty conscience . . . for he who promised is faithful.

I don't care what life you've lived or how many heinous sins you've committed. If you've dedicated your life to God and truly serve the Lord Jesus, you can pray in confidence! Some translations of Hebrews 10:19 use the word "boldness." Picture yourself boldly coming before Jesus seated on his throne. Do you understand what this means? No matter how hard Satan tries to condemn you, you can refute his lies! You can pray for whatever is on your heart and know that God is listening. We have that privilege!

There is also a second part of righteousness, though. Living righteously means conforming to God's standard of right and wrong. It means making a decision to live out the principles in the Bible. We cannot live life our way and expect God to answer our prayers. "The LORD is far from the wicked but he hears the prayer of the righteous" (Proverbs 15:29).

We are not perfect! In Romans 7:9 Paul wrote that the things he wanted to do he didn't do, and the things he didn't want to do were the things he found himself doing. Isn't that the truth! We are flawed people. No matter how we try, we can never live a perfect life, not on this side of heaven. That's why it is so awesome that our righteousness is based on what Christ has done! Thank God he doesn't expect perfection!

Faith and righteousness go hand in hand. Righteousness is faith being lived out. True faith in the Lord will lead to righteous living. We can't claim to have faith in the Lord and live life our way. Fully surrendering means making a conscious decision to walk under the direction of God, as he would have us live. At the same time, our righteousness comes by faith in Christ. The English word "righteous" originated from an old Anglo-Saxon word, *rihtwis,* which meant *right wise.* The Old Testament Hebrew word that is translated as "righteous" means *lawful,* or *clean.* Both of these have to do with the idea of right choices.

Repentance and Confession

Because of our sinful tendencies, confession and repentance need to play a large part in our prayer lives. Repentance means making a decision to turn around and go in a different direction. It's not just feeling sorry for your sin, but determining to change! Understand that confession of sin does not bring about forgiveness. We don't fall out of forgiveness every time we sin. Forgiveness is included in our position in Christ. Once we've given our lives to the Lord, we are forgiven for all our sins, past, present, and future. But confession and repentance are important in keeping us humble before the Lord and keeping our lives on the track God intends. I picture our lives like a car. If you take your hands off the steering wheel it will begin to veer, be it ever so slightly. Eventually, you'll be going totally in the wrong direction. Confession is like keeping our hands on the steering wheel. It keeps us on the right path!

I almost always begin my prayer time with "soul searching" and confession. I ask God to put a spotlight on my life and bring to mind areas where I need to confess to the Lord. Sometimes nothing needing confession comes to mind. Sometimes it does. It may be a sinful thought or a wrongly spoken word.

I remember one incident that happened to me years ago before I was married. I had a friend staying over for the night and the two of us had a bit of a heated conversation. We both then went to bed mad. Before I dozed off I decided to pray. I opened my Bible to Matthew 5. There, in verses 23 and 24, Jesus tells us that if we're offering a gift to God and remember an offence we have against another person, we're to leave the gift, fix the offence, and then come back to offer the gift to the Lord. I got out of bed and went into my friend's room. To my surprise, she was crying. I apologized to her and we made up. I needed to clear that offence up before I spent time with God. I was a young adult, but that left a clear impression on me of the importance of being right before the Lord when I pray!

Once I have confessed and set things right, I can continue in prayer knowing that I am cleansed. I remind myself that my position in Christ gives me the right to pray! If the enemy has tried to convince me there is an area of my life that makes me unworthy to enter into prayer, in faith I take back that territory. I do this by specifically standing against his lies. I will often verbally claim scriptures that support my spiritual right as a follower of Christ to enter into prayer. Two of my favorites are James 5:16 and Hebrews 10:19-22 (quoted above).

Be aware that attacking our worthiness to approach Christ is one of the primary methods Satan uses to try to destroy our prayer lives. It's not unusual for him to whisper how sinful we are and try to bring a feeling of condemnation. "Again, you fell!" "You'll never overcome this!" Scripture refers to him as the "accuser of our brothers, who accuses them before our God day and night" (Revelation 12:10). I've prayed with countless sisters and brothers in Christ who are so caught up in these particular lies of the enemy that they feel unworthy to pray. What a liar Satan is! Of course we might need to alter our life choices, but as we understand our position in Christ, we can and should be bold in our prayers in the throne room of God!

For others Satan brings the lure of self-confidence and pride. Their focus is solely on their relationship in the Lord and they've neglected the righteous living the Word speaks of. They need to choose to follow the principles of the Word of God and determine to make life changes. How can the Lord answer our prayers when we are not living in a way that pleases him?

Both of these lies are dangerous and need to be severely dealt with in order to have an effective and dynamic prayer life.

Public or Private Confession?

There are occasions when we need to confess publically before others. I've seen this misused, however. We're not expected to, nor should we, confess *all* our sins publically. We need to be wise in this area. If you're led to confess to others, I recommend finding a Christian you trust to honestly share with. I've seen people confess things that were totally inappropriate and not helpful, either for the person confessing, or for those hearing them. One man confessed sexual sin that had occurred many years ago to a room of mostly children, many of whom were his Sunday school students. Another confessed sin in a church service that should have been confessed in private. None of these people ever asked or even told the pastors or leaders of their intentions. They were acting out of condemnation and guilt.

There are times, though, when we do need to publically confess our sins and shortcomings to others. It's important to first ask a pastor or leader you respect and trust for direction and counsel.

A time of confession and repentance should also be included in a group prayer meeting. It's a good idea to give a time of quiet reflection before people are asked to pray. Ask God to put a spotlight on the lives of those in the room. Offer the possibility for confidential confession to a trusted leader in the prayer group. Unconfessed sin will hinder prayer, both personal and corporately.

When we really understand the concept of righteous living, both in our positions in Christ and our daily life choices, tremendous freedom comes into play. Our prayer lives are able to rise to an amazing level. God is honored, we are blessed, and results are seen!

Discussion Questions

The prayer of a righteous man is powerful and effective. (James 5:16)

1. How would you define a "righteous" person? How would God define it?

2. How would you define "powerful and effective" prayers? What kind of results would you expect from them?

3. What is the difference between positional righteousness and righteous living?

4. Which of these two concepts is harder for you to grasp, and why? Has difficulty with these concepts ever tripped you up when you tried to pray?

5. What role does the grace of God play in this chapter's principle ("The prayers of the righteous are powerful and effective")?

6. Why is confession essential to an effective and powerful prayer life?

Prayer Action Step

How can righteousness play a more active role in your prayer life? Do you need to spend some time in confession to the Lord? Or do you instead need to be reminded of your righteous position in Christ? If you've never surrendered your life to the Lord Jesus, this would be a great time to do that!

If you're studying in a group, share your personal thoughts and struggles concerning righteous living. Pray for one another. If you're doing this study alone, describe the changes you may need to make in your journal and then ask the Lord to help you live them out.

Chapter 6

Principle 5:

WE NEED TO LISTEN AS GOD SPEAKS TO US

WHEN WAS THE LAST TIME YOU'VE PERSONALLY heard from God? I don't mean in a vague, distant way; I mean *personally*? Do you hear the Lord speak to you? This should be commonplace both in our lives in Christ as well as when we pray. Listening to the Lord is completely linked with having an effective prayer life. Without it, we're not praying as we should!

Listening for the Lord's Leading

I learned an important principle many years ago that's guided me throughout most of my Christian life. *Not every good deed is God-led.* Let me put it this way: just because something is good to do doesn't mean it's the will of God for you. I've learned not to assume doing or giving something is the best choice unless I've sought the Lord for direction.

I remember a man who attended our church many years ago. He was single and had a very good job. The amazing thing was that the time came when he lacked sufficient funds to pay his basic bills! He finally came to my husband and shared how he was giving all his money to homeless men, one in particular. How could that be wrong? Now, giving money to the poor is a great act. But in this case it was not God-driven.

This is where hearing from the Lord plays an important role in our Christian lives. Without truly listening to God, our prayers are ineffective. We need to take steps under the direction of his sovereign leading. That takes committing our ways to the Lord and listening to him for guidance. This is walking by the power of the Spirit. When we don't walk under the leading of the Spirit of God, we're walking by the flesh. When we're not praying with the intention of listening and following the voice of God, we're praying in the flesh. It's that simple! I don't care how good an option may seem: when we act according to our own understanding, it's not God-blessed. Because of this, we need to cry out to the Lord for clarity and guidance and listen intently for his leading.

Faith plays an important role here. Is God who he says he is? Is his Word real? "My sheep listen to my voice; I know them, and they follow me." I take these words from John 10:27 literally. I listen for his voice, then I follow his leading. He's not going to expect me to follow when I can't hear him. I know that in spite of the fact that I'm a pretty dumb sheep at times, God is able to convey his will to me in a way that I'll recognize. I place my trust in him, not in my limitations, and stand in assurance that his grace is working in my life.

SURRENDER.

When I'm seeking direction, the first thing I do is surrender. That may sound simple, but it's the most important part of hearing from the Lord. I remember that when other kids would taunt me as a child, I would put my hands over my ears and yell, "I can't hear you!" I get that picture of us sometimes when we're asking God for direction! We have to give God full control, with the attitude of "Whatever you say, Lord, I will do!" We need to trust that as Philippians 2:13 promises, "It is God who works in you both to will and to do for His good pleasure" (NKJV).

WAIT.

After I've surrendered, I wait. Trusting is the key here! I've talked to some who are seeking God's direction with a "we'll see" kind of attitude. It's like they're waiting with their arms crossed saying, "I'll see how much I can trust him!" It's as if God has to somehow prove he's in control. Where's the faith in that?

How long do I wait? Until I receive an answer. If deadlines come, I let them pass. I heard a great teaching about this from Charles Stanley many years ago. He stressed that we should never let deadlines determine our decisions. If God hasn't revealed clearly what to do, keep waiting till he does. He'll show us at just the right time!

LISTEN AND EXPECT.

And finally, I listen and expect. As I study the Bible, I open my heart to any direction he may lead me. I'm sensitive to his voice. My ears are tuned to him and my heart is open to his leading. Can you see the freedom this brings? I can have joy in the waiting because I know I'm where I should be for this time. If and when he wants me to move, he'll make it clear.

> If any of you lacks wisdom, he should ask God, who gives generously to all without finding fault, and it will be given to him. But when he asks, he must believe and not doubt, because he who doubts is like a wave of the sea, blown and tossed by the wind. That man should not think he will receive anything from the Lord; he is a double-minded man, unstable in all he does. (James 1:5-8)

I love God and I know he loves me more than I can ever imagine. My security is in the fact that God never has and never will let me down! At the right time, he will make the way clear. My role is to wait and listen. When fear or the dread of "what ifs" enters my heart, I stand against it. God is in control! He is sovereign. He knows my limitations. I know he wants the best for me and my desire is to serve him, so I stand in faith and peace. Trust me in this; God's will is not a hidden treasure. He will make it clear at just the right moment.

When He Speaks

I love to hear from God! There have been times when He has spoken to me so clearly that to doubt would be sin. Sometimes he speaks to me through a verse in Scripture. It will almost literally jump through the pages at me. I remember one time when I sensed God was speaking to me concerning a particular chapter in the Bible. It was a mighty word of blessing and favor. I asked, "Lord, are you really speaking to me through this chapter? Can I really claim these words?" I recorded all of this in my prayer journal. That evening we visited a church service and the pastor preached a sermon based on a verse-by-verse study of the very chapter I had read that morning. I sat in tears as I was ministered to by God in a powerful way.

Some of his words have come through others, maybe through a sermon or a song. There have been times when others have shared a "word from the Lord." How I appreciate it when brothers and sisters have obeyed the leading of the Lord and shared these messages with me. But I can honestly say that the times I've heard the Lord's voice the most was in the quiet of my prayer times alone with him. Sometimes the words come with a sense of his presence so strong that I don't want to move. I hardly want to breathe. Other times his voice is just a knowing, an awareness. I don't hear from the Lord every time I pray, but when I do, it is more than special to me. When he speaks to me it's often through what people describe as "that still small voice" (see 1 Kings 19:12, KJV). It's an awareness of information. I just know that I know! Scripture teaches that "his sheep . . . know his voice" (John 10:4). I recognize his words, be they ever so soft!

I remember when we first moved to Houston. We were doing church planting, so needless to say our money was more than tight! About a quarter of a mile from our house was a small strip mall with a large corner room for rent. The Lord began to minister to me to claim this place as our place of ministry. I remember arguing with the Lord that it was impossible. "Are you sure I'm hearing you? Are you sure?" I have to confess that I doubted God in this. It was so far beyond what we were able to do! However, I shared this information with my husband and we began praying for this place and claiming it as ours. For the first few weeks I regularly drove into the parking lot, either alone or with others, and thanked the Lord for it, praying for protection for the building and blessing for our future ministry.

As the weeks turned into months, my times of prayer for this possible opportunity began growing farther and farther apart. Soon

I was barely praying and in several months, I gave up. One day, as I drove by, the Holy Spirit spoke as clearly as if he was sitting next to me: "When did I tell you to stop praying for this building?" I confessed my sin of unbelief to him and began claiming it again! Within six months we were renting this property. What a blessing it has been in our ministry! I have to tell you, the best part was not the building, but seeing the miracle of how God provided and knowing he spoke it into my life! What a joy to hear from the Lord!

There are times when we need to pray in faith without constant reassurance from God that what we're praying for is in his will. As I pray, I ask the Lord for guidance. Many times he confirms his leading through Scripture, agreement from another Christian brother or sister, or another way of his choosing. There are those times, though, when I need to pray solely according to how I sense he's leading me. During these times, I trust him to redirect me if I'm not praying on the right path. I remind myself that his strength is made perfect in my weakness, that he knows my flaws and human boundaries, and that his ability to work things together for good far outweighs any of my human limitations. The important thing is that I want his will, I'm fully surrendered to him, and I understand my role is that of a tool in his hands. My desire is to completely follow his leading. The answer depends on him and him alone!

It's as if we're coming before the Lord with our prayers and leaving them at his throne. We're saying, "God, this is what I believe you want done in this situation. I trust you to answer as you see fit. I trust you! Show me if there's something I'm not seeing. This is all about you." That, my friend, takes both faith and hearing from him, as we lift our requests to the Lord.

I believe every person who serves Christ should hear from him. I have seen this principle misused, however! I was in one meeting where "the voice of God" spoke through nonbelievers giving direction for the church. This was not only accepted but encouraged! I've been in other meetings when a person was "spoken to from God" and frankly humiliated in front of the church body. There've been times when a brother or sister has shared a "revelation" they've received from God that I knew was not his voice. I knew this either from the content of the message or because of the details I knew about the person's life. I have to tell you, I seriously doubt the validity of these "messages from God."

Why We Don't Hear

That being said, Christians should truly hear from the Lord. Unfortunately, too many Christians have thrown the baby away with the bathwater on this subject. Why don't we hear from the Lord more often? Here are some reasons.

We may not be listening.

How often do we come before God and never give him time to speak? Our focus is so much on sharing what's in our heart that we don't listen to what he has to say! We need to train our hearts and minds to listen to him. Learn to spend time in quiet meditation. Don't feel the time has to be filled with constant talking or even worshipping. Learn to listen!

This includes corporate prayer times. Have you ever noticed how awkward people can feel when no one prays for a few minutes or even seconds in a prayer group? A person will often pray out just to end the deadly quiet. Silence is perfectly fine! Allow people to sit reflectively and in quiet meditation. Honestly, though, this is not natural, either when you pray alone or in a group. It takes training to break this habit of constant chatter. I guess we need to slow down and learn to listen!

WE'RE NOT EXPECTING HIM TO SPEAK.

It shouldn't surprise us when God does speak to us. The book of Acts tells us that the Spirit told Philip to go stand next to a chariot with a eunuch sitting in it. I personally don't think Philip heard an audible voice. I believe the Spirit spoke to Philip through that still small voice, and because he had trained himself to listen to God's voice, he heard and obeyed. Later he introduced the eunuch to the Lord and even baptized him.

Hearing from God should come as no surprise. After all, we were made for fellowship with God. Who do you know who ever experiences fellowship without mutual communication?

SOME HAVE DOCTRINAL VIEWS THAT AFFECT THEIR HEARING FROM GOD.

Many believe the Lord *only* speaks through the Bible . . . period. They don't believe God will speak a prophetic word either through others or personally. I heard one man teach that God never speaks through dreams. Granted, we need to be careful and discerning when hearing the voice of God, but I strongly disagree with the conclusion that God will never speak in these ways. After all, he is God! He's spoken in these ways throughout the Bible and I don't read anywhere in Scripture that he's ever stopped.

Still others believe the Lord will almost *always* confirm his voice or will through a prophetic word. Both views limit people hearing from God. The key here is balance. Does God speak through the Bible? Yes. Does he speak a prophetic word? Yes. But those are not his only options. He is God. Remember he spoke through a donkey to a prophet named Balaam in order to get his point across!

A few years ago I was getting ready to check out at a local grocery store. I sensed the Lord leading me to go to a particular line with a very grouchy woman cashier. For a few seconds I fought it but soon obeyed and began checking out my food. I asked her how her day was going and she responded, "You don't want to know!"

"I really do," I assured her. She began to pour out her heart about how taken for granted she felt by her husband! The Lord miraculously gave me words to minister, and she and I were both deeply blessed. She was blessed by the fact that someone cared and hopefully by some helpful words, and I by the pure joy of being used by the Lord! How did I hear from the Lord to go through her line? It was a prodding. It was like the Holy Spirit was pushing me, ever so gently. I've learned to step out at these times. I usually say a quick prayer and ask Jesus to lead me.

Sometimes I don't see a positive result of my actions or words. Just because we don't see fruit doesn't mean it didn't happen. That's okay; I follow what I sense is the Lord's leading and I leave it on the altar. The Lord works in mysterious ways. We don't always have to see what he's doing. That's his business. Ours is merely to obey.

I remember another time of hearing the Lord's voice several years ago. During my early-morning prayer time, I was praying for a couple in our church that was getting ready to deliver a baby. The pregnancy seemed to be going well. I found myself deeply burdened to the point of tears. I began praying for them and crying out for the safety of the child. All at once I yelled out, "I take authority against that umbilical cord!" I'll tell you, the words surprised me as they flowed out of my mouth!

A few hours later, my husband called and informed me that this couple had delivered their baby. I asked him if there were any complications and he told me he didn't think so. I did not tell him about my prayer burden for them. We hung up the phone. Not five minutes later he called me back and said the husband had called and told him that the umbilical cord had been wrapped around the baby's neck several times. He said it was a miracle the child was uninjured. I began to weep in thanksgiving that once again I heard and responded to the voice and leading of God!

MANY PEOPLE DON'T HEAR MORE FROM THE LORD BECAUSE THEY DON'T SPEND ENOUGH TIME IN PRAYER AND BIBLE READING.

They just don't spend enough time with God! Think about it: how is it you can recognize a person's voice? It's not from studying *about* her; it's from spending time *with* her. Isn't that true? We recognize God's voice by taking the time to get to know him more. It's as simple as that!

This doesn't seem to be a very popular line of thinking today. In days gone by, it was a common teaching for Christians to spend a daily time in prayer and Bible study with the Lord. It even had little nicknames like "quiet time," "QT," "devo time," etc. Today, though, it's almost not politically correct to discuss this. The emphasis is on flexibility. Maybe some Christians think spending a daily time with God is too legalistic. I'm not sure why, but I do know that Christians spend much less time with God every day than they did in years gone by. Of course we're having a hard time recognizing God's voice. It's being muffled by our own busy lives.

God loves being with us. I remember a song by Larnelle Harris called "I Miss My Time with You!" It's written from the perspective of how God misses us when we're too busy to be with him. It's true. After all, he's our "Abba Father." He loves us like a daddy would.

Way too many Christians try to fit a time with God into their day, if they spend time with him at all. The better option is to fit our day around our time with God! Try making choices based on that. You may need to cut back on some activities. Draw a timeline of your day. What can be penciled out? Where does the majority of your time go? Maybe you need to turn the TV off and go to bed earlier at night so you can get up and pray before you go about your day. You may need to invest in a good alarm clock and learn to set it! One choice I've made is not to turn my computer on before I've spent time with the Lord. Without a doubt something draws my attention away from God and before I know it, time is gone!

I've always had my prayer time in the early morning hours. I'm one of those crazy people who actually enjoys getting up really early. I love getting up before anyone in my house and even my neighborhood! I realize not everyone is like me, but I can assure you there is a time for you. You need only to discover it. When something's a priority we will go out of our way to do what ever it takes to accomplish it. Let's make our times with God that priority.

People don't hear from God because they don't recognize his voice.

You've probably heard this old story. It had been raining for many days, and a man was stuck on a roof. As the waters rose, the man faithfully prayed for God to save him. As the flood levels began to rise, a rowboat, then a speedboat, and then a helicopter all came to save him. He refused help from all and drowned. Standing before the Lord, he asked why God hadn't answered his prayer for safety. God gave him a puzzled look and replied, "I sent you two boats and a helicopter. What more did you expect?"

What are we listening for? What do we expect God to sound like? Some of us want writing on the wall, or a ground-shaking thunderbolt. God has never chosen to speak to me like this. He can if he wants to; after all, he is God. But I have never, personally, heard him speak this way!

It amazes me how often Christians, women in particular, have a hard time hearing the voice of God, yet are more than open to listening to messages of defeatism, failure, and poor self-worth that come from within. They have listened to these messages for so long that they no longer recognize them as lies. For some of us, these are leftover inner recordings of negative messages we've been told by our parents throughout our lives. For others, a negative thought may have been embraced from a traumatic emotional event.

Whatever the reason, these self-condemning themes constantly play over and over again in our minds and are often lived out as truth. I wonder how long a person would remain friends with someone who continually spoke unkind, condemning words. My guess is not long. Yet we continue to listen to these lies from within! The commandment tells us to love others as we love ourselves. Some of us need to begin loving and accepting ourselves more and stop listening to these childhood prerecorded messages! Maybe the voice of God is being shouted out by the condemning thoughts from within.

One thing to consider is that God tends to speak within our personalities and particular gifts of the spirit. He has made us diverse and those differences are what make the body of Christ so blessed! He never expects us to mimic each other. For some, he might choose to speak through Scripture. That tends to be the way my husband usually hears from God. For others, a timely prophetic word comes into play. For people like me, that inner voice becomes the spoken tool, often during, but not exclusively, in my prayer times. He will speak to us in his way according to who he is and what he wants us to know. Don't worry: he will speak. The question is, are you listening?

Discussion Questions

My sheep listen to my voice; I know them, and they
follow me. (John 10:27)

1. What are some common ways God speaks? How do you recognize his voice?

2. Can you think of a time when God has clearly spoken to you? How did you know it was God speaking?

3. What is meant by the statement, "Not every good deed is God-led"?

4. There are many good things you are capable of doing. How can you know which of them God is leading you to do?

5. What should you do when you're not sure of the voice and leading of God?

Prayer Action Step

Begin journaling about the times when God speaks to you. Be specific about what you've heard as well as the date you heard it. If you're not sure, write it down anyway. In time, you'll discover whether you're sensing him or your own impressions. As you read over these entries, you may be amazed at the times God has spoken to you through various ways.

If you're studying in a group, break up in groups of two or three and pray for one another, that each will grow in sensitivity in hearing his voice. If you're studying individually, ask the Lord to help you learn to hear his voice more.

Chapter 7

Principle 6:

PERSISTENCE IN PRAYER BRINGS RESULTS

M AYBE YOU'RE LIKE ME—I want everything done yesterday. I hate to wait! I TiVo any program I watch because commercials frustrate me. I seldom start long projects. I hate reading long books because I want to know the ending now! So the idea of being persistent in prayer, or "praying through," is not an easy principle for me. It is exciting, though, when I've seen the Lord answer a prayer, even though it seems to have taken a long time to answer. Praying through a prayer burden to a place of victory brings an amazing reward of inexpressible joy.

Our society is a "now" society. We want everything quick and easy. Our food is microwaved, our TV programs are TiVo'd, and we carry phones with internet connections for immediate information. Everything is done right away! Unfortunately, we often expect the results of our prayers to be instant too. We don't want to wait for anything, least of all an answer to prayer from God.

How Long Should We Pray?

How long should we continue to pray for a prayer request? My answer to that is until the Lord removes the burden or until we experience the victory. There are several prayer burdens I carry that I have been praying for over several months and in some cases years. I go through times of doubting whether these are really from the Lord or prompted by my own desires or thoughts. When these periods of doubt happen, I continue to pray and ask the Lord for wisdom. God knows my limitations and he will lead me.

Be assured that there is no such thing as wasted time spent in prayer. God will use the time to mold, teach, and bless us, not to mention answer our requests! He will use it for good in our lives as well as in the lives of those we're praying for. Personally speaking, I have been blessed most by God during times of waiting. These times cause me to keep my eyes on him. I've learned to trust him and his sovereignty. For some of us, "praying through" is when we stop kicking and screaming and learn to surrender and trust.

When we don't see any answers to a particular prayer after an extended period, it may be wise to come before the Lord again and ask him to confirm that it is his will for you to continue with that particular prayer burden. Ask him for a scripture that you can hold on to as an anchor while you continue to pray for this. God has blessed me with awesome portions of Scripture during these times. Sometimes he's lifted the burden and has led me to focus my prayers in a different direction. Other times he's confirmed his will to keep praying, through a particular scripture or a word of encouragement from another believer.

But there have also been times when I've just known that continuing in prayer was the right thing to do. The book of James teaches us that if we lack wisdom, we should ask God and he will give it, but we need to be careful that we're asking in faith, and not wavering. If we're not sure, bring it before the Lord and ask for clarity and discernment. He'll make things clear to you. Certain prayer requests are sure things, though, like praying for the lost. This is always in God's heart! You can pray these prayers with certainty.

There's a teaching in the Christian community that says we should pray once, and then leave it on the altar. It's kind of a "tag it and bag it" idea. I've heard it said that if you revisit a prayer request you're not acting in faith, that real faith is praying once and then leaving it alone. I couldn't disagree more. Often the key to victory is praying through to the end. It's holding on and not giving up. We may need to remind ourselves that we're in it for the long haul and that we're in a spiritual battle. During these times, I speak the words that I am claiming the victory and I am not giving in. I remind myself that I'm running the race all the way to the finish line, and that includes my prayer life!

Prayer Weapons

The enemy hates it when we pray through to victory. When persistence in prayer is needed, I'll often pray through the weaponry found in Ephesians 6:

> Finally, be strong in the Lord and in his mighty power. Put on the full armor of God so that you can take your stand against the devil's schemes. For our struggle is not against flesh and blood, but against

the rulers, against the authorities, against the powers of this dark world and against the spiritual forces of evil in the heavenly realms. Therefore put on the full armor of God, so that when the day of evil comes, you may be able to stand your ground, and after you have done everything, to stand. Stand firm then, with the belt of truth buckled around your waist, with the breastplate of righteousness in place, and with your feet fitted with the readiness that comes from the gospel of peace. In addition to all this, take up the shield of faith, with which you can extinguish all the flaming arrows of the evil one. Take the helmet of salvation and the sword of the Spirit, which is the word of God. And pray in the Spirit on all occasions with all kinds of prayers and requests. With this in mind, be alert and always keep on praying for all the saints. (6:10-20)

I like to take on the different weapons listed and describe what each one means in a particular situation of prayer. For instance, if I'm praying for a pressing financial need I may pray, "I take on the belt of truth! I know the truth of the Word is real. God is my provider; he will provide my needs. I take on the shield of faith. I stand on the faith that Jesus is in control of my finances. I will not give in to fear." And so on for all the weapons listed in this chapter . . . the breastplate of righteousness, the helmet of salvation, having my feet fitted with the gospel of peace, and the sword of the Spirit.

Never forget that you are in a spiritual battle. Scripture teaches us that we're not fighting against flesh and blood, but angels and powers. I've learned through the years how true that is! I remember one vacation our family took almost twenty years ago. We went to upstate New York in hopes of spending a few days enjoying time alone with our family. Unfortunately, much of our first day was spent in quarreling and bickering, not only between our sons, but between my husband and me as well. That night seemed to last forever. We all had a very disturbed night of sleep.

It was the next morning when Danny and I began comparing notes that we realized we were under spiritual attack. Now I don't like to see a demon under every bush and I sure don't want to give Satan more credit or attention than he deserves, but I also don't want to be blind to the obvious. Satan was behind this and we needed to pray specifically against him! We gathered together and prayed against his actions. We prayed for the peace and presence of the Lord to take control of that hotel room. I cannot begin to tell you how differently things went. The anger and agitation left and there was peace. Since that time we pray for the presence of the Lord to control every hotel room we stay in. God only knows who was there before us and what kind of situations were practiced. And we never want to experience another vacation like the beginning of that one!

Don't Give Up!

Consider the teaching of Jesus from Luke 18:1-8, the Parable of the Persistent Widow.

> Then Jesus told his disciples a parable to illustrate how they should always pray and not give up. He said: "In a certain town there was a judge who neither feared God nor cared about men. And there was a widow in that town who kept coming to him with

the plea, 'Grant me justice against my adversary.'

"For some time he refused. But finally he said to himself, 'Even though I don't fear God or care about men, yet because this widow keeps bothering me, I will see that she gets justice, so that she won't eventually wear me out with her coming!'"

And the Lord said, "Listen to what the unjust judge says. And will not God bring about justice for his chosen ones, who cry out to him day and night? Will he keep putting them off? I tell you, he will see that they get justice, and quickly. However, when the Son of Man comes, will he find faith on the earth?"

I love this teaching. To me, Jesus is saying, "Be bold! Be persistent!" Never give up on a prayer burden. No burden is too small or too big. If it's important to you, it's important to God. When a need is pressing on my heart I will lift it up to the Lord as often as I think of it. This is especially true if it's something that's bringing a negative emotion like anger or fear. Every time the thought comes to my mind, I say, "Thank you, Lord, that you're in control of this." I then specifically pray about my pressing need. I literally picture myself coming before the Lord's throne on a consistent basis, bringing my request before the Lord. Along with coming before the Lord throughout the day and keeping my focus on Him, this also prevents me from allowing the enemy to bring negative feelings into my life. Those feelings never work for good and I need to take them captive!

As I mentioned earlier, I love Hebrews chapter 11. It's by far my favorite chapter of the Bible. I've read that chapter more times than I can count. I was amazed and humbled, however, when I read and really understood verse 13: "All these people were still living by faith when they died. They did not receive the things promised; they only saw them and welcomed them from a distance." Did you get that? Not one of these great heroes of faith ever received an answer to their prayers. They never received the promises that God had given! They died in faith believing God would answer their requests and give them the promises due them. Their promises were fulfilled, but these wonderful saints never saw their fulfillment—not on earth, that is. As I sit here writing these words, I don't know if I could ever be so faithful. I can only hope! I see now why they're listed in this chapter of faith. What great examples they are to me!

Combating Doubts

Persistence is one characteristic Satan will try desperately to break down. He does not want you to carry through in prayer. He will encourage you to question the validity of the prayer. "Is that *really* possible?" "Does God *really* want that?" And my favorite, "Did he *really* promise that?" He is such a liar! One thing is important to keep in mind: the enemy usually mixes in a bit of truth with his lies. He'll speak enough fact to make you doubt. He's a pro at this. But remember, partial truth is still a lie. Truth is truth! I always told my sons a person may speak the truth fifty percent of the time, but you can never fully trust his words. How do you know which fifty percent he is speaking?

The enemy will remind you of your shortcomings and how many times you've prayed for this particular prayer need. He'll throw in a bit of confusion, and before you know it, you're questioning whether you should continue with your prayer.

I remember a time not long ago when I was being bombarded with negative thoughts about a particular person in my life. These thoughts were really affecting how I prayed for this person. Some of the thoughts were based on truth, many on lies. But they left me confused and worse, afraid! I came before the Lord and asked for clarity. I asked him to remove the confusion I was experiencing. I have to admit that it took me several weeks of praying and crying out to God for this need. But glory to God, he answered my prayer! It was like the picture came into focus and I knew how to pray for the other person! I realized the negative thoughts and fears were attacks from the enemy in an attempt to discourage me from praying. I saw this, continued praying, and saw the victory in both the other person's life and mine!

Negative thoughts are one of the main ways Satan will try to discourage you. How many times does he whisper the projected ending of a situation before you've even started in it? You face discouragement before you've taken even one step. Second Corinthians 10:5 reminds us that "we demolish arguments and every pretension that sets itself up against the knowledge of God, and we take *captive* every *thought* to make it obedient to Christ."

Our minds are a place of battle. If our enemy can influence the way we think, he wins a great victory. I love this quote from material from Scope Ministries: "A lie believed as truth will affect your life as if it were true—even though it is a lie." How many times have I spoken with a person who's living a very limited life based on lies! Time and time again, I hear words like, "I can't, I never will." Often these are complete lies that the person has bought into. That's where the belt of truth and the sword of the Spirit come in to play. It's important to know the Word of God to combat Satan's lies!

We Need Each Other

The body of Christ plays an essential role here. To put it bluntly, we need each other! Sometimes we are tag team pray-ers. Just when we're ready to throw in the towel and stop praying for a particular need, someone else will say something that encourages us. We may need to share a burden to ask for prayer support too. In each case, we need support from other Christians! One thing to keep in mind is that if the Lord has given you a particular prayer burden, he may not have given to others. Don't be discouraged if those you share with are not as excited as you are. Some burdens from the Lord are personally for you.

Be discerning about sharing your prayer requests. It's not always wise to blurt them all out in public prayer meetings. It's great to find a prayer partner or someone who you trust to be discreet and confidential. They may discern that a burden is obviously not from God when you may not be able to see it. I've experienced this several times with young adults carrying a "burden from the Lord" to marry a certain person. Others would have been helpful in seeing the errors of this "burden."

Following the Leading of the Lord

There are times when we need to stop asking God and start thanking him for the unseen victory. This prompting will come from the Lord and then we must trust him to lead. As I shared before, this was the case when I prayed for our meeting room! It got to the point that when I prayed for God to provide this place, I was convicted. I needed to take the next step to not only thank him for it but to also ask for guidance as to what to do with it once we were meeting there! Again, I didn't hear any audible voices telling me this, I just knew it. The Lord will guide you during these times of persistence in prayer. He may speak through Scripture, maybe another person will shed some light, or maybe you'll just know! Remember, a key to praying through is listening for his leading.

It's important to note that as we act on the leading of the Lord, it gets easier the next time to recognize his voice. As we hear from the Lord and remain consistent in our prayers, things are often not quite so foggy the next time. Our day-by-day experiences are stepping-stones for the bigger leaps of faith when the Lord will call us to pray for a tougher situation. Don't forget Principle 2: *God exists*. Again, it's essential that we see and acknowledge the day-by-day interventions of the Lord so that we will have the faith for the more difficult ones. I don't know how many times I've been faced with a challenge to pray through on an issue and I was reminded of another time I stayed the course. This gave me encouragement to keep trusting and praying.

All these principles work together. As we remain persistent about a particular burden, we need to be listening for the leading of the Lord and then stepping out in faith. You cannot separate one principle from the others. They're all connected!

Look at God and Not the "Doors"

There's a particular idea among Christians called the "open-door policy." This belief says that if there's an open door it must be the Lord's leading; a closed door shows that the Lord must not want you to go this way. I've found quite the opposite to be true. Often, Jesus leads us to pray open a bolted door! He may want us to stand against that closed door in faith. That's where perseverance and hearing from God come into play. I don't know about you, but I don't think Abraham was seeing too many open doors when it came to sacrificing Isaac. He just stepped out in faith.

And not every open door is an invitation to enter. There have been many times I was glad I did not go through a seemingly open door. As I was able to look back in hindsight, it would have been a grave mistake! It often takes prayer, listening to the leading of the Lord, and accountability to others to know what to do. One thing is for sure, though: if you seek the will of God, he will lead you in his time!

This really hit home when my husband, the senior pastor of a church we were working in, was heading up a huge building drive. There was no way we had all the money we needed to build this church. But the Lord was clearly leading in a very step-by-step way. One time in particular, we needed $150,000 within a two-week period and we didn't have it. I mean we didn't have *any* of it. We committed it to the Lord and kept going. The door was not open—there wasn't even a door to be seen—but we were pretty sure the Lord wanted us to continue. The days came and went and still no money. It wasn't until the night before the due date that my husband got a phone call. The Lord had provided the needed money! This became a stepping-stone for some future times which were even more challenging. Our faith and persistence grew in leaps and bounds.

Praying for unsaved loved ones is one of the hardest yet most important areas we need to persevere in. I've talked to countless Christians who have basically given up on praying for unsaved friends or family. They're convinced this person is beyond hope and the door is closed. No person is beyond hope! Where there's breath, there's hope. Keep praying and asking God for leading as you do pray. Christian author and speaker Kay Arthur prayed for many years for the salvation of her son. Many share in similar testimonies. Keep praying. It's worth it.

Hebrews 11 finishes with the words, "These were all commended for their faith, yet none of them received what had been promised, since God had planned something better for us so that only together with us would they be made perfect" (11:39-40). God withheld the answers for *our* benefit! He has provided something better for us. We get the blessing of discovering how God eventually did answer the prayers of these precious saints. I don't know about you, but I feel very special!

Discussion Questions

> All these people were still living by faith when they
> died. They did not receive the things promised; they
> only saw them and welcomed them from a distance.
> (Hebrews 11:13)

1. The saints mentioned in Hebrews 11 prayed in faith, often for many years, without seeing the answers to their prayers. How do you think they were able to persist? How can you follow their example?

2. What is the longest stretch of time you've ever prayed for a particular request? Have you stopped lifting up this request? Why or why not?

3. How does persistence in prayer run counter to our culture and lifestyle? Why is it hard to persist in our society?

4. How can Scripture help you to persist in prayer?

5. Why is being connected with a body of believers important to persisting in prayer?

Prayer Action Step

List at least three practical steps you can take to make persistence a reality in your prayer life. Maybe you can share your requests with others more often, or perhaps rediscover through Scripture God's heart toward your particular prayer burdens.

If you're studying this in a group, spend some time brainstorming possible ways to make your prayers more persistent. If you're studying this independently, make a list and commit it to God.

Chapter 8

Principle 7:

GOD HEARS THE PRAYERS OF THOSE WHO CRY OUT TO HIM

THROUGHOUT THE BIBLE, GOD OFTEN led his people to cry out. Time and time again he led them in battle this way. Think back on when Joshua directed his people, by the power of God, to collapse the walls of Jericho. How did they do this? Joshua 6 tells us that God brought down the walls with a shout.

Have you ever wondered why he had the people shout? Of all things to have them do, why that? Because lifting our voices takes faith. Sometimes just stating facts aloud validates the reality of whatever the situation is. It somehow makes it real. Have you ever deliberately not spoken something out loud in the hope that silence would keep it from being true? I know I have.

The Old Testament is not the only place that speaks of crying out to God. "During the days of Jesus' life on earth, he offered up prayers and petitions with fervent cries and tears to the one who could save him from death, and he was heard because of his reverent submission" (Hebrews 5:7). If Jesus cried out to God, I do believe we should too.

Someone recently asked me if we need to pray out loud or if it's enough to pray silently. Of course God does hear us when we pray silently, but I encourage people to pray out loud for several reasons.

Praying aloud helps make our times with God more interesting.

Our prayer times should be powerful and *enjoyable*! Praying aloud keeps them from falling into the category of the mundane or purely mental. We should never pray simply because we know we should; we should also pray because we love this time with our creator God. These times with God should be something we can't wait to have. God wants to meet us when we pray. Now that's exciting!

Praying out loud helps keep our focus on God.

Let's face it: we're human. I can't tell you how many times I've been praying and found myself planning my dinner menu, including writing down a list! It's so easy to become distracted, and before we know it, our time is gone. When I'm struggling with a drifting mind during my times with the Lord, I'll often sing my prayers. I make up a tune to words that I want to pray. I do this to get myself over the hump of my distracted thinking. If that doesn't work, I'll try reading Scripture aloud. I'll also spend time listening to worship music. I determine not to allow my undisciplined mind to control my prayer life. I take the control, and if singing my prayers or reading Scripture helps, so be it.

It's easy to quit praying when things get tough. Consider the night Jesus was betrayed. He left three of his disciples to pray and watch as he poured out his heart before God. What did he find when he returned? They were sleeping. They weren't able to focus and stay awake for even one hour to pray! I'm sure they did not know it was one of the most important nights of their lives. I wasn't there that night, but I wouldn't be surprised if a bit of praying aloud or even a song or two might have been a big help!

Praying aloud professes words of faith.

Romans 10:9 says it's not enough to believe in your heart Jesus is Lord; we also need to confess with our mouth that God raised him from the dead. There's a spiritual blessing that comes with speaking words of faith aloud. I recently heard a preacher say that we need to proclaim a positive future. He went on to quote Psalm 23:6: "Surely goodness and mercy shall follow me all the days of my life" (KJV). I so agree with this. We can be sure the Lord always wants to work things together for good in our lives. "'For I know the plans I have for you,' declares the LORD, 'plans to prosper you and not to harm you, plans to give you hope and a future'" (Jeremiah 29:11). His mercies are new every morning.

Like many other good insights, the idea of speaking words of faith aloud has been distorted. I've heard it said that we have to be careful what we say because Satan will hear our words and use them against us. Although we do need to be careful of the words we speak, I don't go that far! That can easily lead to paranoia. Should we then write our messages to one another for protection? Or better yet, should we all join a silent convent? This seems a bit drastic to me! That being said, our words do matter. We have to be careful of the words we speak. They do make a difference in our lives.

This is true when we pray, too. It's important to verbally declare things, especially things of faith. Not only do we need to hear the profession of faith, but the enemy needs to hear it coming from our mouths. Every time Satan tempted Jesus in the wilderness, He rebuked him out loud and declared the truth verbally. He could have just turned his back and ignored him. But he took another route. He lifted his voice aloud.

Why should we be any different? When God has spoken a clear promise to me, I will declare it when I pray, and I will always do this out loud. If God has promised me protection, I will pray, "Thank you, God, for the protection you are giving me, right here, right now!" Am I praying for an unsaved loved one? I may pray, "Thank you, Lord, that you love this person more than I ever could. Thank you that your hand of mercy is on her life!" Often, just hearing my own words increases my faith. It may sound a bit crazy, but I verbally remind myself and all angelic and demonic beings that the victory is mine!

Praying aloud is encouraging to others.

Have you ever been encouraged hearing someone else verbalize victory over a prayer burden? I have. Just hearing another's profession of faith will spur me on to keep my eyes on the Lord and to trust him to bring victory.

For some of us, our personalities come into play. We may be more the quiet type. Maybe we don't want to feel awkward. Not all of us are wired as David was when he danced before the Lord in (basically) his underwear. Although I don't believe all of us will be people who will shout out in groups of people, I do believe we all should be willing to lift our voices to him. We can limit what God can do through us by not being willing to leave our comfort zone. Many of us are more than willing to shout at sports events but shun the idea of showing any emotion in prayer and worship. You never know what God has in mind or how you could encourage someone else.

Have you ever asked yourself what stops you from crying out to God, really crying out to him? I think sometimes it's not realizing our desperation for the Lord. If you were in a situation where you felt desperate enough, I do believe you'd cry out for help. For example, if you saw a child running toward a street full of cars, I can venture to say all of us would scream for the safety of the child, either for the child to stop or for someone to intervene. When we pray, do we really see how desperately we need God's touch in the different situations we're praying for? Maybe we should ask God to show us this need clearly.

What a joy to lift our voices to God! We should never allow our prayers to become too mental and routine. Again and again Scripture exhorts us to cry out to the Lord. I take that literally. Our desperation for him often comes through as we lift our hearts, our hands, and our voices up to our creator God. Lift your voice to him! Believe me, he'll never put you down for it and you may really enjoy it! The blessings far outweigh the discomforts.

Discussion Questions

During the days of Jesus' life on earth, he offered up prayers and petitions with loud cries and tears to the one who could save him from death, and he was heard because of his reverent submission. (Hebrews 5:7)

1. According to Hebrews 5:7, Jesus cried out in prayer. Why? How does it make you feel, knowing Jesus did this?

2. What are some common obstacles to praying aloud? Which ones make it hard for *you*? What can you do to overcome them?

3. How might praying and crying aloud as Jesus did become part of your prayer life?

4. How can spoken words be a blessing in your Christian life, including your prayer life? Can they be a hindrance sometimes? Why or why not?

5. What are some creative ways you can lift your voice to God?

Prayer Action Step

What is the main obstacle that prevents you from crying out to God more? Is it your personality? Is it fear or insecurity? What changes can you make to allow this principle to take root in your life? Also consider your attitudes toward calling out to him. All these and more affect how we cry out to the Lord!

For those praying in groups, share your reservations about calling out to God and pray for one another. For those studying alone, be sure to make note of any hindrances to lifting your voice more to him and be sure to write them in your prayer journal.

Chapter 9

Principle 8:

WORSHIP IS ESSENTIAL

I F THERE'S ANYTHING THAT HAS RESONATED in this book, I hope it's this: *prayer is all about God.* We can pray eloquent prayers and spend countless hours praying, but if we haven't grasped that basic reality, it's fruitless. It is all about God, period! It's not about us! Because of this truth, we need to base our prayers on worship of him. Simply stated, worship is both a deep-rooted awareness that God is God, as well as a choice to completely surrender to him.

Worship Means Surrender to God

I remember the first time I noticed something interesting in the story of when Abraham sacrificed Isaac in Genesis 22. As he was leaving his servants at the foot of the mountain, with every intention of sacrificing his son, he told his servants to wait there and that he would return after they "worshipped the Lord." After they worshipped the Lord? He was planning to kill his son. How in the world could he consider that worship? But it was, in its purest sense. He was obeying God. He was fully committed to that and nothing, not even his own common sense, would deter him from it. This is an essential part of worship. We cannot worship God and still continue living life our way. It just doesn't work like that!

When I think of worship, one word comes into my mind: surrender. Paul wrote, "Therefore, I urge you, brothers, in view of God's mercy, to offer your bodies as living sacrifices, holy and pleasing to God—this is your spiritual act of worship" (Romans 12:1). Prayer and worship are intricately connected. You cannot have fruitful prayer without worship. They go hand in hand.

I can't begin to tell you how many times I've prayed for something and haven't received what I've prayed for, at least not by my way of thinking. Let's face it, not all our prayers will be answered in the way and time we may expect them to be. What do we do when this happens? I know what many of us do. We get frustrated with God for not answering us. We may either doubt him or the validity of what we're praying for, and in some cases we just give up praying for this burden. But is this really the solution? And what does worship have to do with all this?

Worship has everything to do with it!

Earlier in this book I described the faith of the great heroes of faith in Hebrews 11. I pointed out how they did not receive the answers to their prayers. But they died content and honored by God by being mentioned in his Word. Do you know why? Because their hearts were focused on God! Their eyes were fixed on him. They were worshipping the Lord.

I remember when the Lord first began prodding me to write this book. You'll never know how much I fought the idea. I gave him all the many reasons why that was a complete impossibility. The funny thing is that all this happened several mornings while I was spending time with the Lord in prayer. How could I continue to worship him with this defiance? I couldn't! I eventually surrendered and told him that against all logic, I was willing to do whatever he wanted me to do. What happened next was amazing! Fear was replaced with excitement and anticipation. I began to get excited about the possibility of affecting others' prayer lives. My heart was filled with joy and praise. I was worshipping the Lord in a powerful way!

But you have to know that all this happened *after* I surrendered my fears and insecurities to him. I chose to worship him in obedience to his leading. Logic might tell us that this yielding should happen after the joy and worship occurred, as result of it. But it didn't. I first needed to let go.

Who You're Worshipping

When I enter into prayer, I begin by acknowledging who it is I'm praying to. I thank him aloud and verbally list his attributes. Who is this great God? What is he capable of doing? What great miracles has he already done? How has he affected my life? I often include singing during my times of worship. I sing songs that reflect who God is. Of course, as I earlier mentioned, I spend time in confession and self-reflection.

But I basically begin with the concept that I am before the creator of the universe. He loves me. I am his. He has given me every right, through my relationship with him and the resurrected power of Christ, to come before him in this time of prayer. I am able to enter with confidence and lift up literally any request that is pressing on my heart. I'll tell you, it's better than any therapy session. I pour out my heart before my creator God for whom nothing is too difficult. And you know what? I have his full attention! How awesome is that?

Praise and Worship

A major part of worship is praise. You cannot truly worship the Lord without praise, and praise without true worship is empty. Both are essential for an effective prayer life. Psalm 22:3 says that God inhabits the praises of his people. That means that God is present when his people praise him. But many people confuse worship and praise.

Praise is thanking God for what he's done. We can do this in a variety of ways. We can praise him with our words, either through songs or spoken words. We can also praise him with our physical bodies. In the book of 2 Samuel, David danced before the Lord (2 Samuel 6:14). In the book of Timothy, Paul encourages all to "lift up holy hands in prayer" (1 Timothy 2:8). Other forms of praise include painting, interpretative dance, and drama, to name a few. Praising God with our whole selves, including our bodies, is an awesome experience!

Praise in general means making positive statements about someone; in this case, it's God. Praise is giving adoration to God. Praise is something we do and say. It's part of our worship. *Worship* is surrendering to who God is. It's acting out devotion. Worship involves total surrender. When we worship, it's more about who we are in relation to who it is we're worshipping. I recently read that the opposite of praise is criticism but the opposite of worship of God is blasphemy! That has a lot of truth.

Both praise and worship are essential to a powerful life of prayer. Worship must be involved throughout our prayers. The basis of worship is surrender. The essence of our prayer life is also surrender. How can we think of praying without the constant reminder of who it is we're praying to?

Luke 19:37-38 describes the time Jesus entered into Jerusalem: "The whole crowd of disciples began joyfully to praise God in loud voices for all the miracles they had seen: 'Blessed is the king who comes in the name of the Lord!'" Although the people did not fully understand the relationship they could have with Jesus and had not yet fully committed their lives to him, they were praising him for what they'd seen him do. As important as that is, worship goes deeper. Worship engulfs our praise. Worship does not just involve thanking him for what he's done; it's surrendering to him for who he is! It's a commitment of devotion to him.

I have to confess: it disturbs me to see Christians choosing to live lifestyles completely opposed to the teaching of the Word of God, yet freely praising God. I've seen many willfully living in sin, with their hands raised and faces beaming. Now I love praising God. I also love seeing others praise him, but my deep desire is to see all worship the Lord in spirit and in truth. And that involves surrender.

In the greatest commandment, God told us to love the Lord with all our hearts, souls, and minds. This is the essence of worship. It's laying everything down for God and driving our lives with this passion. When our prayers reflect this worship they become powerful. Our focus is on God and his presence fills our lives. He is glorified and we are blessed!

Discussion Questions

On the third day Abraham looked up and saw the place in the distance. He said to his servants, "Stay here with the donkey while I and the boy go over there. We will worship and then we will come back to you." (Genesis 22:4-5)

1. Why do worship and prayer complement and support each other?

2. How is obedience linked with worship? with prayer?

3. What is the difference between praise and worship? How are they alike? Can you have one without the other?

4. What is meant by the phrase "the opposite of praise is criticism but the opposite of worship of God is blasphemy"?

5. Do you agree with the statement "Worship is acting out devotion"? Why or why not? If you agree with the statement, how can you act out your devotion to God in worship?

Prayer Action Step

Think of the main place where you personally meet with God. Is this place private enough for you to praise and worship freely? Can you think of a better place and/or time more conducive to open worship?

For those in a group, share some ways you enjoy praising and worshipping the Lord and then spend some time praying for one another. For those studying alone, spend some time praising and worshipping God and thank him for who he is and how he's working in your life. Enjoy your time of worship with him!

CONCLUSION

WHAT DO YOU WANT FROM YOUR PRAYER LIFE? More importantly, what do you want from God? As I close this book I'm burning with the desire for those of you reading it to see beyond your life situation and to reach out and touch the hem of Jesus. He has so much more for you—more than you could ever imagine—but it's up to you to take the first step!

Bring Your Needs to Him

What is it you need? Are you in need of healing? He's the great physician. Do you feel you're at the end of your rope, hopeless? His mercies are new every morning. Are you lonely, discouraged, feeling confused? He can meet your needs. No request you could ever bring before God is either too great or too insignificant for his touch. If it matters to you, you can be sure it matters to him. "Cast all your anxiety on him because he cares for you" (1 Peter 5:7). That includes everything!

Whatever struggles you're facing, God is able to use them for good and bless you beyond words. The key is taking your eyes off your situation, daunting as it may be, and fixing them on him. It involves trust and, as I've written, surrender!

The best part of surrendering to God is not what he can do for us but through us. There is a world full of hurting people who need the touch of the Savior, and God can use you, through prayer, to make that eternal difference. Do you understand what this means? Your life can count for something beyond your little world! God has plans to use you in a powerful way and your prayer life is pivotal to that!

Keep On Praying!

We in America have redefined "the normal Christian life," and it's more like a downgrade. Our "normal" prayer lives are no exception. When did God ever tell us to stop praying for the sick, the helpless, and the lost? Since when is it perfectly fine to spend little, if any, time with God on a daily basis? Who are we to think that because we've chosen to fill our lives with time consuming "stuff," that's okay with God, that he'll understand somehow? I can assure you, it's not okay, and he doesn't understand. Scripture is loaded with commands to put God first. Jesus demands our full commitment to him, and this includes our prayer lives.

The best part of this is that not only will we see lives radically changed, marriages mended, bodies healed, but we will be blessed as a result. The fact of the matter is that when we pour out, we are filled!

If you're reading this book looking for a sense of purpose, begin praying! As you take that step toward becoming a person of prayer, God will lead you in the "hows" and "who fors." His longing is not only to hear from you but also to speak to you. You can be sure this is one desire of your heart he will fill.

The Lord has an amazing life in store for us. He will meet us in prayer. His presence is available. Who knows what miracles we will experience in our lives? Not only is it possible to see the dead rise, the lame walk, and the blind see, but it's happening, all over the world—maybe not within our Christian circles, but it is happening! Although I have never personally experienced seeing a person rise from the dead as an answer to prayer, I have spoken with missionaries from around the world and American pastors who have.

I don't know about you, but that excites me. I want to be used by God. I want my life to mean something! My daily prayer is that my life will be a poured-out offering to him.

I challenge you to incorporate these eight principles of prayer into your life. Study and memorize them. Make whatever adjustments you have to in order to put God first. And then expect him to do the impossible in and through you!

As I close this book, this is my prayer for you. Feel free to fill in the blanks with your name.

Father God, thank you for who you are! Thank you, Lord, that with you nothing is impossible. I worship you for not only what you do in our lives, but for who you are. Lord, you are the awesome God! Even the stones cry out in worship of your name. You are majestic beyond all understanding.

Father, I pray for _____. I thank you for him [or her] and ask that you use the words of this book to do an amazing work in his life, a work above and beyond anything that either of us could ever ask or even imagine! Fulfill him,

Lord. Lead him. Guide him. I pray for his heart to be stirred with a passion to be used by you through prayer like never before. Lead him to other people of prayer. Bless his daily times of studying your Word. Give him an unquenchable desire for you. Allow him the grace he needs to fight his way through any crowd around him in order to grab on to the hem of your garment. Use his life in a powerful way. Thank you, Lord, that the prayers of the righteous are effective and powerful. It is in Jesus' name that I boldly pray! Amen.

Discussion Questions

1. Which of the eight principles has had the most positive effect on your prayer life, and why? What changes have you seen in your life while reading this book?

2. Describe which principle is the hardest for you to live out. Why? What changes can you make to live out that principle?

3. What needs have you neglected to bring to God? What is stopping you, and how can you change that?

4. How has God encouraged you through reading about these eight principles of prayer? Can you see ways your prayer life could be transformed?

5. List some concrete changes you plan to make as a result of what you've learned from this book.

Action Step

Jot each of the eight prayer principles down on an index card and commit to memorize them. Remember God intends to bless you and, more importantly, to use you to be a blessing to others in ways you can never imagine. Expect these blessings!

Whether you're studying this in a group or on your own, spend an extended time in prayer. Ask the Lord to move mountains so that you will make deep growth changes in your prayer life. Ask him to help you imagine how he might use you when you are surrendered to him. Thank God for the ways he will work in and through you as you grow in.

The Ministry of

BARB HO

www.theultimateconnection.org

Barb Ho is available to speak on various topics including prayer.

If you're interested, or have any questions feel free to email her at

barbho@theultimateconnection.org
or contact her through her website
www.theultimateconnection.org.

JOIN US IN MINISTRY

"Religion that God our Father accepts as pure and faultless is this: to look after orphans and widows in their distress and to keep oneself from being polluted by the world." (James 1:27)

Ministering to orphans in Ukraine has been a passion for Barbara and Danny Ho for many years.

If you'd be interested in finding out more about our ministry to the orphans in Ukraine, please visit our website

www.kindsamaritan.org.